To Doug

MIRACLES DO HAPPEN . . . . .

GOD BLESS !!

MIRACLE MARCIA

KIM RAMBACHER

www.xulonpress.com

Marcia (Latin meaning):

You carry on for others with joy. You have a receptive nature and may bear burdens for others. You are pragmatic, thorough, strong-willed, practical and stubborn at times. You are hard-working, often a martyr to duty. You like home and security above all.

DEDICATION

For Danielle, Pete, Alexandria and Colby

Ryan, Katie, Michael and Matthew

Jordan, Ardelle, Savannah and Keaton

The Korcyl and Rambacher Families

Everyone in the small village of Bemus Point,
New York knows the Rambachers. In addition
to working, Kim is an officer in the Bemus Point
Volunteer Fire Deptartment. His wife Marcia
works in the local high school's main office.
They are always in the stands cheering on the
school's sport teams, especially when one of
their three children is playing. The Rambachers
are active members in their church, and are
loved and respected by all. Living in a close knit
community surrounded by family and friends ...
everything is going so well for this middle
class family.

Their lives take a tumultuous turn in 1998 after
Marcia was diagnosed with breast cancer. Time
after time small miracles surround Marcia in her
seventeen year battle with this disease. In this
book Kim reflects on how he met Marcia, how
they fell in love, settled in Bemus Point, raised
their family, and how they dealt with her sickness.
Apparent through it all is Marcia's strength, faith,
optimism, sense of humor, and continued love of life.

Miracle Marcia is an inspiration to anyone struggling with cancer, to caregivers, and to people of faith everywhere. It reminds us that EVERY day is a gift.

"Marcia – Our sister, our teacher. Her strength and perserverance was truly an inspiration to us all. She taught us the importance of our faith in the Lord.
We love you Marcia and thank you!"
Lanny, Sue, Ed, Greg and Ginny
Brothers and sisters of Marcia

"How richly blessed of God I was, and others that Marcia took with her on her travels through the Valley of the Shadow. Though ordinary in many ways, God gave her extraordinary grace and faith to impact the lives of many for the Lord Jesus Christ. Marcia now lives on the other side in the presence of Christ, her Savior, overflowing with utter joy and complete fulfillment."
Pastor Clyde Mohl
Lakeside Bible Chapel, Bemus Point, NY

"Although Marcia wasn't a certified teacher she taught me so much every day. Marcia taught me about strength, compassion, and living everyday to its fullest. Marcia's wisdom and advice continues to give me strength. I am so blessed to have had her in my life."
Mrs. Julie Verdonik
Principal, Maple Grove Jr. Sr. High School

"Our best friend Marcia was the epitome of fortitude and courage." As in Luke 1:37, "For with God nothing shall be impossible."
Chip and Cindy Swanson
Good Friends of Kim and Marcia

TABLE OF CONTENTS

INTRODUCTION

As Marcia's life with cancer unfolded, there were so many unusual events that surrounded her journey. Our friend and author, Ned Ward said, "These occurrences taken singularly would be an oddity, but together they make a very compelling story."

Marcia said to me, "When this is all over Kim, you have to go back to work and work hard." I knew I was going back to my job, but somehow I also knew that she meant a different kind of work…it was the work that she couldn't finish. She still needed to touch more lives. This book is for you, Marcia, in hopes that your work continues.

CHAPTER 1

THE BEACH LETTER

"Tune your ears to wisdom, and concentrate on understanding."

Proverbs 2:2

April 19, 2015

I was sitting in church trying not to cry. It was a warm, sunny spring day, but I felt so alone. I missed Marcia. Dave Everts, a church usher handed me an envelope. Inside were Marcia's obituary and a letter from a total stranger...

March, 2015

It has been one month since Marcia died. My grief and pain is as raw and real as it was after her Celebration of Life service. What should I do? I wasn't scheduled to return to work until early May. Should I stay close to home with my three children, six grandchildren and Marcia's 96

year-old mother? Should I get away to reflect on the great
life Marcia and I shared? One thing was certain. Marcia
would want me to heal.

As it turned out, the best man at our wedding invited me to
Florida. Denny Martin and his wife Jana asked me to spend
three weeks with them in Indian Shores, Florida, relaxing
at the beach and playing golf. Also, getting a chance to
reminisce with our maid of honor, Marcia Schultz, seemed
like good medicine for my heart.

Marcia Nolan Schultz, the maid of
honor at our wedding 42 years ago
lives in Lakeland, Florida, and was
unable to attend Marcia's memorial
service. With my wife's obituary,
Celebration of Life program, and
prayer card in hand, Marcia Schultz
and I sought solace on the beach
at Indian Shores. We remembered

Marcia Nolan Schultz
and Marcia, July 1990
at the Maple Grove
High School 20th
class reunion

'Miracle Marcia'. Walking the beach, we laughed, cried,
and struggled with the fact that life would go on without
her. We eventually returned to the beach chairs. I realized
that the paper mementos of my Marcia's life had blown
away. We searched the sand and shoreline, but found only
two of the papers. Her obituary was gone.

We never found the obituary. Someone else did. Her name is Cindy Davin, a vacationer. She read it and returned it to my pastor. Her letter to me reads…

"Dear Mr. Rambacher,

You don't know me, but my name is Cindy and last week while on the beach in Indian Shores, Florida, I picked up a crumpled and torn piece of paper and put it in my bag without looking at it. When I got back to my condo, I took it out and noticed that it was perfectly cut and not just a torn piece of newspaper blowing in the wind on the beach.

I was so conflicted on what to do with it. Did a family member leave it there on purpose because that was a place that Marcia loved and had so many memories? In which case, I should put it right back where I found it. Or, did someone carry it with them as a memento of Marcia (as I often do with mementos of my mother who passed less than three years ago), and it slipped out of their bag by accident?

I thought about it for a few days and decided to do my best to return it to you or whoever brought a memento of Marcia to Florida from New York. The two deciding factors that made me want to return Marcia's obituary were:

1. *My circumstances for being in Indian Shores: Before the September of 2013, I had never heard of Indian Shores. We have a friend who has a brain*

tumor and our community held a benefit for him to raise money for medical bills and to help the family when he passes. A live auction was held for the larger items that were donated, and my husband and I just kept bidding on a week at Indian Shores until everyone else stopped, because it was for a good cause. I was meant to be there that day and in a way, to meet your lovely wife and learn the story of her life.

2. *I had a difficult time with the passing of my mother and I love to get signs from her. Mine happens to be butterflies at all the right times and in all the right places! If this is your first sign from Marcia, then I am honored to have brought it to you and I can promise you that it won't be your last.*

May you find peace and comfort during this very difficult time for you and your family. What a beautiful life Marcia lived in this world, and your family was so blessed to have her, if even for such a short time. So with that said, I return this as a sign from Marcia to her husband, children, mother, grandchildren and siblings that she is with you and always will be."

Cindy Davin, Pearl River, New York

Wanting to hear more from Cindy, I phoned her a week later. She told me that she had found Marcia's obituary four days after it had vanished. Tangled in sea grass, it lay only 20 feet from where Marcia Schultz and I had been sitting that day. Coincidentally, Cindy and her husband had stayed at the same condo complex where I vacationed.

As someone once said, "There are no accidents...there is only some purpose that we haven't yet understood."

BEMUS POINT, NEW YORK – Marcia Frances Korcyl Rambacher, 62, a lifetime resident of Bemus Point, NY, passed away peacefully with her family by her side at 10 a.m. Tuesday, February 3, 2015, as she entered the home of the Lord with great expectations and excitement.

Marcia was born June 5, 1952, in Jamestown, NY, a daughter of Sophie M. Evanczik Korcyl and the late Stanley J. Korcyl.

She was a 1970 graduate of Maple Grove Jr.-Sr. High School, and following graduation had worked at the Weber-Knapp Company for seven years. She then took some time off to have her three beautiful children, then proceeded to work for 30 years at the Maple Grove Jr.-Sr. High School. There she worked as a teacher's aide, librarian assistant, and attendance officer. Her kindness, smile and caring for her fellow workers drew people toward her.

Marcia was a devoted member of the Lakeside Bible Chapel in Bemus Point for 34 years. She was well loved at the church and gave her love to all her brothers and sisters of the Lord Jesus Christ.

The Lord used Marcia with his miracles and inspiration as a carrier to lead many people to him. She touched so many people with faith, optimism, endurance and her fight to win this game, which made her the best athlete of life. Her 17-year battle with this horrific cancer didn't change her attitude about her love of family, friends, her co-workers and staff at Maple Grove High School. Marcia leaves behind a family and a community who mourns her loss, while celebrating her eternal life in Heaven.

CHAPTER 2

SHOCKING NEWS...PART I

"God hides his most precious treasures
for his saints in their most difficult and
painful experiences."
Things Not Seen - Jon Bloom

Marcia and I were lying in our bed on a May morning. Suddenly she rolled over and brought her hand up to her breast. "Kim, there's a lump. Feel this."

I felt the thickening in her right breast. A wave of fear passed over me, tempered somewhat by the possibility that it could be benign. I asked, "Don't you have a mammogram scheduled?"

"Yes, this Tuesday," she answered.

The mammogram results were troubling. Dr. McCormick took me aside and told me there definitely was a mass. He didn't know if it was cancerous, but said its appearance was suspicious. Everything happened so quickly after that. The doctors were very concerned. A biopsy was performed right away in the office. We were to return the next day for the results.

That night, Marcia said, "Whatever the outcome is, we have to learn to live with what the Lord gives us." She added, "We are not in control."

The next morning Dr. McCormick said, "Marcia, it is cancer and it is a fast growing cancer. We have decisions to make."

I nearly screamed, "NO, NO, NO!" I was spinning out of control. I desperately wanted to sprint out of the doctor's office and keep on running. I was breathing hard. I tried to focus. My mind was a kaleidoscope of wonderful memories.

I needed to talk to the doctor. I needed to support Marcia. Instead, I drifted back to 1968, the year I met Marcia...

CHAPTER 3

PURPLE ROLLERS

*"Love is patient, Love is kind. It always
protects, always trusts, always hopes,
always perseveres. Love never fails."*
1 Corinthians 13:4 7-8

Our story began in the summer of 1968. My family visited Bemus Point, New York for the first time. On a hot August day, Carol Bradley, a relative by marriage, invited me to go horseback riding in the fields off of Bayview Road.

I had never ridden a horse before, and the experience was amazing. When we finished riding, we returned the horses to the neighbor's barn. Carol then said to me, "Come on, you've got to meet my friend."

I followed Carol into an old farmhouse and there, sitting at the table was a pretty blonde in her nightgown. She was getting ready for church, and she had huge purple rollers in her hair. Carol introduced us.

"Kim, this is my friend Marcia Korcyl."

Wow, I thought, she's really something even when she's got purple rollers in her hair!

Two and a half years later I was involved in a student council exchange program. Denny Martin, our class president, our class secretary Tim Carl and I went to observe Maple Grove High School in Bemus Point. What we saw was nothing like our high school in Stow, Ohio.

The 60's were a time of great changes which were vividly reflected at Maple Grove. In Stow, students were required to follow a very strict dress code. Jeans were forbidden and the guys' hair wasn't allowed to touch their ears. The girls' skirts, when kneeling, had to be one inch from the floor.

Given this, imagine our astonishment when we saw Maple Grove's boys with hair down to their shoulders. The girls wore culottes and very short skirts. We concluded that this casual dress code allowed students to be themselves, and therefore more at ease in the classroom.

Later that day as we were walking down the hall with our guide, I saw a blonde walking toward us. Very interested, I asked "Who is that?"

"Oh, that's Marcia," our guide responded.
"Does she live on a hill above Bemus Point?"
"Yes," our guide said. "She lives on Bayview Road."

I remembered that smile! In a flash, the memory came flooding back. The girl I saw walking down the hall was the same girl I had met in 1968. I had ridden her horse, Misty.

Marcia and I attending the Maple Grove
Senior Prom, May 1970

I needed to act quickly! In less than two days my friends
and I were returning to Ohio. I learned that Marcia did
not have a boyfriend, so I started calling her. After several
calls, she finally answered.

"Hello," she said.
"Is this Marcia?"
"Yes."
"This is Kim Rambacher. I was at your school yesterday.
My brother married your neighbor, and would you be inter-
ested in going to a movie tonight?" I asked in one breath.
"I would love to," Marcia answered.

All of a sudden I was nervous and excited. I was going on
a date and I didn't even know this girl. We saw *Mash* and

21

Patton, and then went back to her house. We had a great time, and I could hardly wait to call her again.

Was it love at first sight? It might have been for me. I'm sure it wasn't for her. Unfortunately, I lived in Ohio and we were miles apart. Despite that, I really wanted to see her again.

CHAPTER 4

SOPHIE, SCRABBLE AND THE SLEDGEHAMMERS

"A man that hath friends must show himself friendly."
Proverbs 18:24

After Marcia and I had dated for two months, I met her family.

I was intimidated and downright terrified when I pulled into the driveway and saw a man and three young men knocking down a wall with sledgehammers. The foursome, Marcia's dad and brothers, stopped working long enough to give me 'the look'. I walked past them and thought, "What am I getting into?" I felt guilty when I kept walking by them, but I didn't exactly know what to do with a sledgehammer. Looking up, they said, "Hi," and then got back to work. I walked into their farmhouse, met her mom Sophie, and then we went on our date.

Before I went to Marcia's house again, I asked my mom how I could make a good impression on Sophie. She suggested that if Sophie liked board games, then I should take time and challenge her to a game.

When I arrived to pick up Marcia for our next date I asked Sophie if she would like to play a game of Scrabble. She was so excited, and as we played I relaxed and felt comfortable. Letting Sophie win the first game was my strategy, something I figured I had to do. She wanted to play another game that night, but I was anxious to be with her daughter. She eventually told us, "Go out and have a good time."

Scrabble became a part of our dating ritual. I'd get to Marcia's at 7:00 p.m., play a game of Scrabble, then go on our date. Marcia and I had a great relationship. She was so sincere when she talked to me and other people. I think that's what I liked most about her.

We continued dating after I graduated from high school. I went to Akron Business College and worked thirty-five hours a week in Bath, Ohio. I drove to Bemus Point on Friday evenings, and spent Saturday mornings doing homework.

This routine continued. After dating for a year and a half, Marcia and I broke up. She had met someone at work, and I began seeing a girl in Ohio. It didn't take me long to realize that no one could take Marcia's place. Simply put, I missed her.

A month later, Marcia called me. She was crying when she said, "I want you to come and see me on your birthday."

My birthday was November 6th, and I made sure I was in Bemus Point. By then I knew she was 'THE ONE!' I'm sure she felt the same way. Not wanting distance to jeopardize our relationship, I started looking for work in New York State.

In 1972, I found a job, moved to Bemus Point and lived in my parents' cottage. Marcia and I began planning our future together.

Our wedding day, July 28, 1973

CHAPTER 5

THE HAPPIEST DAY OF MY LIFE

"The man who finds a wife finds a treasure, and he receives favor from the Lord."

Proverbs 18:22

M arcia and I were married on July 28, 1973. We were both 21. Our wedding was at Our Lady of Lourdes Roman Catholic Church in Bemus Point. I had no pre-wedding jitters because I knew I wanted to spend my life with this lady.

The night before the wedding a lot of my Ohio friends were crammed into a room at the Redwood Ranch in Bemus Point. It's a small, very rustic motel. The guys took me out at 1 a.m. and we never got back until 5 in the morning. I forgot to set the alarm clock.

Luckily, we woke up at 10:30...the wedding was at 11! Talk about a panic. Everyone was running around the room. I was putting on my tuxedo as I ran a toothbrush across my teeth. "Ram, it's time to go. We've got to get to the church! We have fifteen minutes!!" they barked.

I didn't even have time to shower. I was standing at the altar with my long, fashionable 1970's sideburns, not knowing I was sporting a five o'clock shadow. Marcia's first words were, "Didn't you shave?"

"I'll explain later," I said.

After we finished greeting guests in the receiving line, I told Marcia that we'd overslept and were almost late to the church. The story got out to our guests that night, and it was quite the joke!

After we honeymooned in Disney World and Washington, D.C., we rented a place in Bemus Point. We lived there until 1976, when we bought the house across the street. We were settling in and life was good.

CHAPTER 6

SUPER BOWL XV-1981

"But I have called you friends: for all the
things that I have heard of my Father,
I have made known to you."
John 15:15

An unusual set of circumstances led to the unlikely opportunity for Marcia and me to attend Super Bowl XV at the Superdome in New Orleans. The Oakland Raiders defeated the Philadelphia Eagles that year. They were the first wild card team to win the Super Bowl. And we were there, rooting for the Raiders.

It all began when I was a member of the Bemus Point Volunteer Fire Department. In 1977 I was in charge of a basketball game that had our volunteers competing against the Buffalo Bills. That night after the game, I met Keith Moody, the Buffalo Bills' defensive back. He and his wife Celia were at the SeeZuhr House restaurant. Keith asked me, "Do you live nearby?"

"Yes, we're living on Alburtus Avenue, two blocks away."

"Do you play cards?" he wondered.

"Yes," I answered.

"Let's leave and play cards, just the four of us."

I remember thinking, "Wow, I'm bringing a Buffalo Bill to my house!" After that night, Keith and I became friends and stayed in touch with each other.

Keith played five seasons with the Bills, but was eventually let go. He was picked up on waivers by another team. When he called to tell me the news, my first response was, "Don't tell me you were picked up by the Oakland Raiders. I can't stand that team."
"Well," Keith said, "you'll have to be a Raiders fan now."
"Okay," I said reluctantly.
He replied, "Make sure you get your airplane tickets to New Orleans."
I reminded Keith of the Raiders' record, two wins and three losses. There was no way they were even going to make the playoffs.
"You and Marcia pray about it," Keith said.

In a small and strange way Keith led us to look closer at our spiritual lives. At one point he gave us a book to read about the end of time as alluded to in 'Revelations'. We started having questions about our faith as we delved deeply into the Bible.

As for the football season that year, the Oakland Raiders made the playoffs. Keith was ecstatic! He continued to call and ask me if I had gotten the airline tickets to New Orleans yet. During one call, he told me that he had two tickets to the Raiders-Browns playoff game in Cleveland. I asked my friend Denny Martin to come with me.

The night before the game, I had dinner with Keith, a few other players, and the team's owner, Al Davis. Game day saw below freezing temperatures. I appeared to be the only one rooting for the Raiders that day. After winning the game, number 26, Keith Moody came off the field and gave me a high five. Denny had to hold me back so the Browns' fans wouldn't maul me! Before we parted ways, Keith told me again, "Get your plane tickets, Kim."

The following week, the Raiders defeated San Diego and cemented their place in Super Bowl XV. The camera panned to number 26 coming off the field. I looked at Marcia and asked, "I wonder if Keith will call tomorrow?" "You know he will, Kim. And you didn't make arrangements yet, did you?"

After working the third shift, I was heading to bed when I heard Marcia coming up the stairs. "Kim, you have a phone call from Oakland."
I grabbed the phone and said, "Congratulations Keith. You're going to the Super Bowl!"
He responded, "You and Marcia are going, too! I have four tickets for you. Can you make it to New Orleans?"
"Of course we can! We'll be there."

Keith orchestrated the whole weekend. When we arrived in New Orleans with Marcia's sister and brother-in-law, we went to dinner with the players. The next morning we ate breakfast with the team and cheerleaders, and then were bussed to the Superdome. Unfortunately, Keith's hand was broken returning a kickoff. The Raiders went on to defeat the Eagles 27-10. After the game, we went to the victory party where 'Celebration' by Kool and the Gang was played over and over again. Marcia and I sat there star struck by the celebrities and VIP's we had met. Marcia always attributed good things to God, and she felt that this too was a gift from Him.

CHAPTER 7

FINDING OUR WAY TO THE LORD

*"And the peace of God, which passes all
understanding, shall keep your hearts
and minds through Christ Jesus."*
Philippians 4:7

In 1983, after Danielle and Ryan were born, Marcia miscarried what would have been our third child.

"This was planned," Marcia told me.

"What do you mean, this was planned? Do you mean that the miscarriage was planned?"

"Oh, yes, that little fetus of mine is in Heaven," Marcia answered.

"Your fetus was only three months old," I replied.

"It doesn't matter. Our baby is in Heaven," Marcia confidently replied.

Her assurance during this emotional time touched me. I began to realize the enormous part our faith was playing in our lives.

Marcia began to accept the Lord when her friend Maureen Stahley took her to the Lakeside Bible Chapel. I could see the changes in Marcia as she reached out to me and other people about matters of faith.

"You have to read the Bible, Kim. That's the only way you are going to get to know Him. It's the right thing to do," Marcia would remind me.

Being baptized by Pastor Mohl, Chautauqua Lake,
May 1984

Marcia was excited when she talked about the Lord to others. Most everyone wanted what she had, a peace that the everyday world couldn't bring.

As I came to accept the Lord, I joined my wife at the Lakeside Bible Chapel. We knew it would be hard to convince our parents that we had found salvation, but not in the Catholic Church. "How could you let your wife do this?" was my parents' response. Sophie, Marcia's mom was the first one to understand. When she and Marcia talked about having the Lord in their hearts, they realized that although our churches were different, we all could know the Lord.

CHAPTER 8

KIM, LOOK UP

"With God, all things are possible."
Matthew 19:26

M arcia and I had visited Hawaii, San Francisco and
Las Vegas. We vowed that when we had children, we
would continue vacationing with them. So in 1993, the
car was packed, and the five of us were ready to leave for
spring break in Madeira Beach, Florida.

The night before we left, my dad called and asked me
to stop at his house. (He and my mom moved to Bemus
Point after they retired.) My mom, Marjorie, was crying
and favoring one side. I suspected that she might have
had a stroke. She wasn't walking well and she was having
trouble with her left arm. Mom agreed to go to the hospital,
but she insisted that we not cancel our vacation.

We were traveling when we learned that a test determined that she had a 99% blockage in one of her arteries.
When Mom had another stroke, we were convinced that
we needed to head home. My sister, Marci, assured us
that Mom was resting comfortably and told us to stay in
Florida. We continued our vacation at Madeira Beach, but

upon returning home discovered Mom was failing. In the end, she was paralyzed after having had seven strokes.

The night before she died, with head bowed I was praying for her. She was in a fetal position in her hospital bed. Marcia stood watch at the foot of the bed.

I spoke to my mom. "Mom, the Lord is with you and he will help you through this transition. I know you'll be seeing the Lord soon. I love you, Mom."

"Kim, look up," Marcia said.

"Kim, look up," she repeated.

As I looked up, I noticed that Mom had raised her hand and placed it on top of mine. Marcia and I were astonished! How was she able to do this? It felt like a miracle.

I couldn't bear watching my mom die. I walked into an adjoining room. Soon a hospital chaplain came to me and said, "Kim, I think you need to be with her."

"No, I don't want to watch her die," I said.

After he left, some presence moved me back to my mom's room. The mood in the room was quiet and serene. Somehow I was given the courage to stand by her side. Mom died a few minutes after I was 'drawn' back to her room. I am eternally grateful that the Lord led me back in time to share the peacefulness of her passing.

CHAPTER 9

GRAND WAILEA RESORT

"Sometimes the heart sees what is invisible to the eye."
H. Jackson Brown, Jr.

In 1994, I won a trip to Hawaii. Marcia and I stayed at the gorgeous Grand Wailea Resort on the island of Maui.

The breathtaking beauty of Maui and our time together was something we never forgot. I remember sitting at a round table in the hotel café. We looked out at the Pacific Ocean and watched the waves roll in and out. The pristine sandy beach, the sounds of the waves – it felt like a dream.

At the Grand Wailea Resort, Maui, Hawaii, May 1995

"Kim, this place is so beautiful. Just think what Heaven must be like."
"You are right, Marcia." Her words stayed with me.

As beautiful as this scene was, Marcia saw it as only temporary. Her spirit focused on her eternal home, one much more stunning than this paradise.

CHAPTER 10

THE HARDEST WORKING MAN

"Do you know a hard-working man?
He shall be successful and stand
before kings."

Proverbs 22:29

Marcia's dad, Stan Korcyl, was diagnosed with stomach and liver cancer in 1997. He seemed fine before dinner on Thanksgiving Day. Later that night, his skin suddenly turned yellow from jaundice.

Stan stood only 5'8" tall, but he was a powerhouse of a man. Being such a hard worker made his illness especially difficult for him. He hated his incapacity.

That Christmas, Stan sat in his chair, smiling and watching his grandchildren. He loved being their grandfather. A while back he told me that my son Ryan was a hard worker, and that he was going to do okay. That was such a glowing compliment from a man of few

Sophie and Stan resting after a hard days work, November 1994

words. He and Ryan had a special bond because Ryan helped him mow lawns.

On January 3rd, surrounded by his family, Stan passed away. Sophie and her eight adult children were devastated. The words of Proverbs 22:29 fit him to a 'T' when I read them at his funeral.

CHAPTER 11

SHOCKING NEWS...PART II

"And I am convinced that nothing can ever separate us from God's love. Neither death nor life, neither angels nor demons, neither our fears for today nor our worries about tomorrow--not even the powers of hell can separate us from God's love."
- Romans 8:38-39

"**K**im! Kim, are you okay? Kim, look at me."

I thought I heard Marcia calling my name. Everything seemed to be happening in slow motion. I shook my head to clear my thoughts. Then I looked at Marcia. She looked pale and worried.

"Marcia, I'm sorry," I told her. It's just that cancer is all so new to me. I drifted away for a few minutes. But I'm here now, Marcia."
"Dr. McCormick, what do we have to do to beat this cancer?" I asked.

Marcia had her right breast removed in June of 1998. Her reconstructive surgery was delayed as they found stage one cancer in her left breast. She had her left breast removed. The reconstruction took place in 2000.

I had a new role. Being a caregiver terrified me. Every day I woke up wondering how Marcia would be. I also wondered how our kids were coping. My emotions were out of control. I worried that I wouldn't be strong enough for Marcia. Fortunately I gathered strength from the Lord, our friends and our church family.

Marcia always reminded me, "I know who's in charge, and it's not me."

Normally Marcia was the pillar of strength in our relationship. However, her self-esteem wavered. After her double mastectomy she said, "Kim, I know that you won't, but if you need to find someone else who is more attractive, I understand."

"Are you kidding me, Marcia? The Lord will get us through this," I assured her. I was echoing the words that she so often spoke to me.

We had a chance to go on a Caribbean cruise later in 1998. Marcia didn't want to go. She had just finished chemotherapy and her hair was starting to grow back. She was also uncomfortable because of her recent mastectomy.

After praying about it, we decided to go. The cruise was great, just like the Love Boat! We both agreed the cruise was exactly what we needed...time together to unwind.

CHAPTER 12

THAT TAKES THE CAKE!

"A wife of noble character who can find?
She is worth far more than rubies."
Proverbs 31:10

When we got married on July 28, 1973, we saved the top of our wedding cake. "We'll have it on our first anniversary," Marcia stated. This tradition is followed by most newlyweds. But I replied, "Why save it for just a year? We are going to be together for a lot longer than that! Let's save it until our 25th anniversary in 1998."

So on our wedding night we wrapped and carefully placed the six-inch square piece of cake in an old freezer at Marcia's parents' house. I'd check on it every other year to make sure it was still there.

Twenty-five years later, over a hundred friends and relatives were gathered at the Maple Springs Fire Hall to help us celebrate our anniversary. Marcia was a little nervous to be the center of attention. She had lost her hair from the chemotherapy. But that night she looked fabulous! She wore a stylish wig, a pale orange dress, and her huge smile.

Our 25th wedding anniversary, July 1998

Our 25 year old cake was thawed for the occasion. Our guests were amazed when they learned that our cake was still intact.

"You try it first, Kim," everyone told me.

The cake looked good, so I tasted a piece. There was still a hint of lemon, its original flavor.

"This is really good, Marcia!"

"Well, let someone else have some," she said.

Slowly a line began to form as our children and family members sampled this piece of history. We smiled at each other as our kids ate a piece of our 'ancient' wedding cake. How blessed we felt to celebrate our 25th anniversary with those we loved the most.

CHAPTER 13

THE ROLLOVER

Angels watching over me every move I make
Angels watching over me every step I take
God only knows the times my life was
threatened just today...
Near misses all around me, accidents unknown
Though I never see with human eyes, the
hands that lead me home.
    'Angels Watching Over Me' - Amy Grant

One night in October 1999, Marcia was driving to Jeanie Shephardson's home to have a cup of coffee. Shortly after she left, I got a call from the Bemus Point Fire Department. I was told that Marcia had been in an accident on Westman Road, only two miles from our house. She lost control on a curve and hit a telephone pole.

Marcia was upside down in her car, and unable to unlatch her seatbelt. She would later tell me that she felt warmth and knew that it was blood running down her face. She said that all she could think about was, "Lord, I have to get out of this seatbelt." Her prayer was answered as she was finally able unbuckle the belt.

Marcia couldn't open the door. She was startled and shocked, and couldn't remember what had happened.

She managed to crawl to the backseat and climb out the window. Once out of the car, she took a few steps, and then realized that she didn't have her hat. She found her way back to the car and grabbed her old denim hat so that she could cover her bald head.

Our good friend Judy Briggs had heard the crash. She ran out of her house to see what the commotion was. Hat in hand, Marcia took a few steps, then collapsed into Judy's arms. They made it to Judy's house, and Marcia was taken to the hospital.

At the emergency room of WCA Hospital, the doctors reported that Marcia had a small cut and a stiff neck. Those who saw her totaled car lying against the telephone pole couldn't believe that she walked away with such minor injuries.

The Lord was certainly watching over Marcia that day. He must have had a plan for her.

CHAPTER 14

FOOTBALL 1998

"No matter what, I'm going to the game.
I don't care how I feel."
     Marcia Rambacher

Marcia always attended our sons' football games. During the Fall of 1999, we drove to Ryan's football game at Alfred University. He was the placekicker on its Saxons Team.

A recent round of chemo had caused Marcia excruciating bone pain. The pain was like clockwork. It started at 8:00 a.m., and subsided at 8:00 p.m. During the game, Ryan was especially concerned about his mom. That afternoon at halftime, Coach Murray told our son to go talk to her. Players never left their team during a game, but Coach Murray knew his player would be more focused after he checked on his mom.

That same fall, Jordan was the placekicker for the Maple Grove Red Dragons high school football team. The team, their families and fans were ecstatic to be heading to Ralph Wilson Stadium, home of the Buffalo Bills, for the sectional championship game. A friend gave Marcia box seats. She and a few families watched the game in comfort. She always loved to see Maple Grove win. And they did, winning a place in the New York State public high school championship games.

A chemotherapy treatment was scheduled for Marcia right before the semi-finals in Syracuse. She knew that she would ache and experience bone pain during the games. Her reaction was, "I don't care how I feel. No matter what, I am going to THOSE games!"

The night before the championship game, several local families got together for dinner. Marcia stayed in the hotel room and soaked in the tub. The next day she was at the game, cheering on her son and his teammates as they clinched the New York State Public High School Section VI Championship! She never let chemo's side effects keep her away from her sons' games.

CHAPTER 15

COMIC RELIEF

"A merry heart does good like a medicine."
Proverbs 17:22

Marcia was scheduled to have reconstructive surgery in May of 2000 at St. Vincent's Hospital in Buffalo. The doctor made marks on Marcia's chest with a pen as she prepared for the procedure. Dr. Neelam, a female doctor of Indian descent, was very direct and didn't mince her words.

"Okay, Marcia. How big do you want them?"

"Wait…" I said.

"Kim, you really don't have any say," Dr. Neelam abruptly pointed out.

Marcia turned, and without a moment's hesitation said, "You're not getting any Dolly Partons this time around!"

"Ah, come on…," I pleaded.

Dr. Neelam assured me that everything would look perfect.

About two weeks after the surgery, we were back in Buffalo for a checkup. Dr. Neelam came into the room, took one look at Marcia and said, "Are you wearing a bra?"

"Yes," Marcia answered.

"Why are you wearing a bra?"

"Because it's part of my clothing," Marcia said. She wasn't sure where this line of questioning was going.

"Marcia, your boobs are so firm, you don't need a bra." When she realized that this garment had outlived its usefulness, Marcia whipped it off right there in the office and threw it in the wastebasket. Shocked and not knowing what to think, I exclaimed, "What the poop!"

CHAPTER 16

THE WAITING YEARS

*"I am going to fight this, but I'm leaving
it in the Lord's hands. Wherever He
takes me on the journey, I'll accept it."*
Marcia Rambacher

Marcia went into remission from 2001-2009, a time I called 'the waiting years'. For eight years after her second breast was removed, she was considered to be in remission. During that time there was no chemotherapy, and she was in relatively good health. Even so, fear that the cancer was still there haunted us each day.

We enjoyed and appreciated every single day. We vacationed and spent a lot of time with our family and friends. We believed that she was given this time to be with Danielle, Ryan and Jordan. It was an incredible gift to be healthy as we attended all of their weddings.

Despite this cancer-free period, in the back of our minds we remembered Dr. Ibaboa's words. He had said to us, "Marcia, when you pass away, it is going to be from cancer."

I understood that he needed to be as upfront and honest as possible. Still, it was tough to hear.

CHAPTER 17

CHEMO...AGAIN

"So do not fear, for I am with you; do not be dismayed for I am your God. I will strengthen you and help you. I will uphold you with my righteous right hand."

Isaiah 41:10

In the fall of 2009, Marcia returned to work as usual. But this time something was terribly wrong. As she climbed the stairs, she was so winded that she could barely catch her breath.

She had to return to Dr. Ibaboa's office because she needed a CAT and PET scan. After reviewing the results, Dr. Ibaboa got right to the point. "Marcia, your cancer has returned. It is stage 4."

The cancer had metastasized from her breast and was now in her lungs, four vertebrae, and there was a spot on her shoulder. Dr. Ibaboa solemnly told us the next steps in her treatment. Chemotherapy would start immediately and he warned us that it would have harsher side effects on her body.

They operated on her lung, performing a procedure called thoracoscopic pleuredosis. According to the experts, pleuredosis is a therapy for lung cancer patients. It removes excess fluid. Five liters of fluid were removed from Marcia's lungs.

Marcia said, "Okay, we will fight this, and the Lord will be fighting it with us." She had determination in her voice as she said, "Kim, don't cry."

CHAPTER 18

THE NUMBERS MAN

*"Whatever you do, work at it with all
your heart, as working for the Lord."*
Colossians 3:23

I had counted stats for Maple Grove's baseball, basketball and football teams for nearly ten years. I loved the job and the kids! In 2010, the Maple Grove Red Dragons basketball team was headed to the New York State Public High School Athletic Association Class D Championships in Glens Falls. That year Marcia's chemo treatments were so harsh that I decided not to go with the team to Glens Falls that weekend. Marcia wouldn't hear of it. She insisted I go.

Before the team left for the game, Scott Kindberg, a sports writer for the local newspaper, interviewed Marcia. He quoted her in the paper saying, "I'm glad he has the stats job while we're going through this. You have to go on with life. You can't just sit in the house. He has been wonderful and gets me anything I need. Some guys can't do this; some husbands can't handle this. He's told me how I inspire him, but he inspires me. I really wanted him to go because he's been at my side ever since I was diagnosed.

I just know that the Lord is going to lead us through this journey."

After winning the state basketball championship at Glens Falls, March 2010. Being home was so special!

Marcia's family stayed with her in my absence, and that weekend Maple Grove won the Class D Basketball State Championship. As the team bus pulled into Bemus Point, there stood Marcia in the crowd that had gathered to greet us. As we hugged, kissed and cried, I leaned into her and whispered, "Thank you for taking care of your caregiver!"

CHAPTER 19

IT'S TIME

*"Behold, God is my salvation. I will trust
and not be afraid for the Lord Jehovah
is my strength and my song. He also
has become my salvation."*

Isaiah 12:2

The teachers and staff got together for a school luncheon in July of 2010. Marcia attended, despite her debilitating neuropathy (numbness) in both hands and both feet. I rolled Marcia, who was hardly able to walk, into the school in a wheelchair. She wore gloves because the nerves in her hands were so severely affected. She had lost a lot of weight and didn't feel well, but she never complained.

As we left the luncheon, I noticed three teachers watching us. "They probably don't think I'll be back," Marcia said. "Oh, you'll be back," I assured her.

"I don't know, Kim. I don't know about this time. It's up to the Lord; it's not my doing."

When we got back home, I helped her onto the couch. She was lying there resting when she said, "Okay, it's time."

"What do you mean?" I asked.

"It's time to get things together," she said.

"What do you mean?" I answered.

"The funeral."

"Really?"

"Kim, we have to do this."

Although I wasn't yet ready to have this conversation, I lay down beside her and she told me her plans. "I want to be cremated, of course, and Pastor Mohl will do the service."

CHAPTER 20

THE FIRST OF MANY MIRACLES

"God also bore witness by signs and won-
ders and various miracles, and by gifts
of the Holy Spirit distributed according
to his will."

Hebrews 2:4

On August 2nd, two weeks after the luncheon Marcia attended at Maple Grove High School, Dr. Ibaboa stopped Marcia's chemo treatments. She was scheduled to have two more weeks of treatment. The doctor feared that more chemo would destroy her way of life. The side effects and neuropathy were very painful. Dr. Ibaboa ordered her PET and CAT scans earlier than planned. He requested that the entire family be in his office when he read the test results. Danielle lived in Charlotte and was unable to be there, but Ryan and Jordan joined us that day.

We dreaded this visit. Was this the end of the line? Would the doctor tell us to start making funeral plans? Was there nothing more he could do?

With all the strength I could muster, I wheeled Marcia into the office with Ryan and Jordan right behind us. We were bracing ourselves for the worst.

Dr. Ibaboa turned toward his patient and asked, "Are you Marcia Rambacher?"

"Yes," Marcia answered.

Looking again at the test results he repeated, "Are you Marcia Rambacher?" Marcia slumped down in her wheelchair and repeated, "Y-e-s." We couldn't imagine why he had asked such a ridiculous question... twice. He knew Marcia.

Dr. Ibaboa then turned to all of us and asked, "Do I have your permission to shout out Marcia's test results to the ten patients in my waiting room?" We looked at each other and all said, "I guess so."

With his back to us, he shouted out to the waiting room full of patients, "Marcia, the cancer on the outside of your right and left lungs is GONE!"

We were speechless. There was more. He continued, "The cancer that was in your shoulder, sternum and vertebras five and seven is just showing up as scar tissue. This indicates it has healed."

"THANK YOU LORD!" Marcia shouted as she tearfully raised her hands.

"I don't understand what has happened," Dr. Ibaboa said. "It can't be explained medically. It's from somewhere else, and Marcia, you know what I'm talking about."

Her doctor, a man of science, had just implied that Marcia's absence of cancer was indeed a MIRACLE!

CHAPTER 21

MARCIA, IT'S A MIRACLE!

*"We have confidence in the Lord that
you are doing and will continue to do
the things we command."*
2 Thessalonians 3:4

Despite the neuropathy in her hands, Marcia reported to work in August. Just a few months before, she had to wear gloves, her hands were cramped from numbness, and she was unable to walk. One of the teachers came into the school office, looked at us in astonishment and said, "You're here! Marcia, it's a miracle!" 'Miracle Marcia' became her nickname.

Marcia hadn't known if she would ever work again. Being able to return to her office and her favorite blue chair meant the world to her.

Marcia remained cancer-free for two years...

In 2012 Marcia went to Dr. Ibaboa's office for a checkup. He told us that cancer had reappeared in Marcia's lung. It was also on the outside of her lung. He explained that it was a milder form of cancer, but it would always be present.

With this new diagnosis and Dr. Ibaboa's blessing, we sought out the Cancer Treatment Centers of America (CTCA) in Chicago. The doctors at CTCA recommended a very specific chemotherapy for Marcia's cancer.

Here we go again...

CHAPTER 22

KINDNESS FROM ALL

"He hath sent me to heal the broken-hearted."
Luke 4:18

S orrows returned to our family in July of 2013 when my sister Marci's husband, Dan died of stomach cancer. Later that year, Marcia's brother Tommy passed away after being diagnosed with pancreatic cancer.

November 6th was my birthday and Tommy's funeral. It was also the day we learned that Marcia's cancer had returned. It was in her lungs, shoulder and vertebrae. Even with the newest treatments, it had spread.

After several rounds of chemo pills, her doctors decided to use an injectable form of chemotherapy. This new treatment lasted six months. She continued to work and rarely missed a day. Unfortunately, she began to lose weight and the neuropathy returned.

Marcia nearly fell down the stairs at our house because her feet were numb. When it happened a second time, I insisted that we sell the house and move. I told her, "I don't want to come home and find you at the bottom of the stairs because you can't feel your feet and have fallen."

We moved into a one story manufactured home which was smaller, safer and nearly maintenance free.

Marcia's coworkers often blessed her with simple acts of kindness. She didn't have enough feeling in her hands to clip on her necklace and earrings. I got into the habit of doing it for her every day. One busy morning, I forgot to do it. When she got to school at 7:15, she noticed that she didn't have her earrings on. She told her coworkers that I had forgotten to help her. Doris Hale looked at her and said, "Marcia, you don't have to worry any more about putting on your jewelry. I'll do it for you." True to her word, Doris put on Marcia's jewelry every morning. If Doris wasn't at school, she would ask Lisa Crandall to do it for her. Such a simple act, yet one that Marcia truly appreciated.

CHAPTER 23

THE LONELY CAREGIVER

"Being confident of this very thing, that he who hath begun a good work in you, will perform it until the day of Jesus Christ."

Philippians 1:6

One morning on my way to work, I heard a report on the radio that discussed the three most stressful events in life. One was the death of a family member. The second was the sickness of a family member, and the third was moving. It seemed unbelievable that we had experienced all three of these events in less than five months.

Stress was taking its toll on me. Caregivers are on call 24/7. Unlike ever before, our world now centered around Marcia and her needs. Caregiving disrupted my life, and I felt I no longer had the freedom to do the ordinary, everyday things I used to enjoy. I longed to take Marcia to our favorite restaurant just to enjoy each other's company. I wanted to travel with Marcia to an exotic beach and watch the sunsets together. At the same time, I longed to run away and leave my responsibilities behind. I battled these feelings, and the profound sense of guilt I felt for being selfish.

Marcia once asked me, "How can you stand the way I look? I'm not attractive anymore. I feel sorry for you because you have had to go through this." In the end, though, my love for Marcia kept me going. Friends and prayers helped me cope.

Caregivers are encouraged to share their feelings. I often talked to Denny and Jana Martin, Tim Carl, and Marcia's friends Cindy and Debbie. I kept in touch with other friends. I often invited them to our home. It kept Marcia's mind engaged. I needed those friends, too. They brought a sense of normalcy to my world.

I'm an amateur inventor. I have created gag gifts that include hairbrushes for bald men and mulligags for golfers. Filling orders for my inventions was a brief but welcome diversion. I was relieved of my caregiving duties if only for a few moments.

People have asked me how our kids have coped with Marcia's illness. It was like a roller coaster ride for them. There were a lot of highs, lows, twists and turns over the years. Jordan, our youngest, lived at home longer than his siblings. It was difficult for him to remember Mom before cancer.

Danielle and her mother had the gift of gab. They were always on the phone. Those mother-daughter talks were definitely therapeutic.

Ryan was a good listener and allowed me to unload on him. He always let his mom know that he was proud of her. He admired her strength, resilience and love of life.

Danielle, Ryan and Jordan were their mother's cheerleaders. They rooted for her, lifted her spirits, and applauded her moves as she played out her game of life.

CHAPTER 24

EARLY RETIREMENT

"To everything there is a season, and a
time to every purpose under heaven."
Ecclesiastes 3:1

"I don't know if I can make it this year," Marcia told me as she returned to work on August 23, 2014.

A week before her scheduled PET and CAT scans, Marcia didn't feel well. As we walked into Dr. Ibaboa's office on October 13th, she said, "Kim, be prepared because I don't think these test results are going to be good."

Dr. Ibaboa walked in and closed the door. He confirmed what Marcia already knew. "Marcia, the test results are not good. I don't want you to work any longer. This was your last day of work. You have more important things to do. You should start getting things in order. When you leave here, you need to go back to school and tell your principal that you are retiring today."

As Dr. Ibaboa suggested, we went to the high school and talked to Julie Verdonik, Maple Grove's principal. "Julie, I have to retire now," Marcia said. With tears in our eyes, the three of us looked at each other. We all knew the implications of Marcia's early retirement.

We discussed Marcia's test results and retirement with our children. All five of us agreed that contacting the Cleveland Clinic was our next priority. We weren't willing to give up.

I called the Cleveland Clinic and was informed that our first step was to get a doctor's referral. After that was processed, Marcia would have an appointment within three weeks. "We don't have three weeks," I anxiously told them. After I mentioned two doctors' names who worked there, Marcia got her appointment.

Two days later we met with Dr. Abraham. He reviewed Marcia's test results. "The tests show that your previous chemo wasn't effective. That is why your cancer has grown. I'm recommending a different type of chemotherapy," Dr. Abraham told us. This was a blessing for us! Marcia had a treatment in late October, and again in November and December.

Marcia wasn't feeling well on Thanksgiving Day. Twenty-four of us had gathered at her mom's house for dinner. As usual, Marcia said grace. This year she broke down during the prayer. She knew it would be her last Thanksgiving.

She continued praying, "I have so much to be thankful for this Thanksgiving...my family, my children and my husband. I've been blessed and I hope my family realizes this. HE is here today blessing everyone. The Lord will help and guide all of you in much the same way he has guided me."

Her prayers at Thanksgiving and again at Christmas were powerful. You could feel the presence of the Lord when Marcia prayed.

Taking a stroll on Kiawah Island,
South Carolina, New Year's Day 2015

CHAPTER 25

KIAWAH ISLAND, SOUTH CAROLINA & CLEVELAND, OHIO

"God's love for you is deeper than the oceans and His presence is everywhere. Whenever you're at the beach, just thank God for His beautiful creation. If His hand has the power to create the seas, then rest assured His hand will guide you and get you through trials in life."
Bible Reasons.com

Who doesn't love a beach vacation? Imagine our surprise when the father of a volleyball player whom our daughter-in-law Ardelle coached, gave us the keys to his home on Kiawah Island! We drove to Kiawah right after Christmas.

Kiawah was so peaceful. We took pictures of the beautiful sunsets. Those sunsets colored the sky with countless shades of pink.

We spent New Year's Eve at Kiawah Island Park. Danielle along with our two grandchildren, Alex and Colby, joined us. A band played 70's music as I wheeled Marcia around the park. She felt so good.

"Don't ever forget this night," she said.
"I never will," I replied, as fireworks lit up the sky.
On January 5th, Danielle and her children left for their home in Charlotte. After Danielle left, I noticed a change in Marcia's mood. She never complained, but she was unusually quiet.

On January 8th, Marcia was very lethargic. She said, "Kim, I'm just tired and weak."
I answered, "Marcia, I think we need to head for home."
"You're right," she said. "It's time to go." After two nights in Charlotte with Danielle and her family, we left for Bemus Point on January 11th.

Now at home, as Marcia rested in her chair, I phoned Sue Verbosky at Hospice. "Sue," I said, "Marcia is really weak. We have an appointment at Cleveland Clinic on January 14th.

As her caregiver, I just don't know how I can deal with this. It's been 24/7 since October."

"I understand, Kim. Let me know how the appointment goes," she said.

Before reaching Cleveland, we stopped at my sister Marci's home. There we visited our good friends, Denny and Jana Martin and Tim Carl. Denny took me aside and told me it was apparent how much Marcia had changed in the last six weeks. Sadly, we all knew that her health was failing.

Marcia, Marci and I left for the Cleveland Clinic. After Marcia's tests, we ate lunch and then headed to Dr. Abraham's office to hear the results. The doctor and his nurse, Nancy, greeted us. He stood next to Marcia and held her hand.

"It's not good, is it?" Marcia asked.

"No, it's not, Marcia. The cancer has grown so much that nothing can help you now. Even the chemo we've been giving you has not helped. We are stopping it as of today. We will be giving you something more for pain." As he pre-scribed more morphine, his nurse held my hand.

Marci wheeled Marcia to the waiting room. I stopped, turned around, and saw Dr. Abraham. I walked up to him and asked, "Doctor, how much time do we have left?"

"Kim, you have less than a month."

"Really?"

"Yes," he answered. I was so shocked I could hardly speak.

I couldn't tell Marcia. I didn't tell anyone. I had to keep this secret. Only Sue Verbosky from Hospice knew.

We dropped Marci at her home and drove back to Bemus Point. When we got home Marcia said, "You know our boys' birthdays are coming up on February 3rd and February 21st. You HAVE to remember that if I die on one of those days, you will be celebrating–their birthday and my first day in Heaven."

CHAPTER 26

CRIES IN THE NIGHT

*"Weeping may last through the night,
but joy comes with the morning."*
Psalm 30:5

Later that night we watched one of Marcia's favorite shows, 'Dancing With The Stars'. At one point Marcia sighed and said, "I don't have any interest anymore."

"That's okay, Marcia," I said.

She looked over at me and said, "Kim, when this is all over, you have to be strong...you can't be a wimp."

"That's easy for you to say. You'll be in Heaven and I'm going to be left here."

"Oh, it won't be long, you'll be following me," Marcia said. For months Marcia had to sleep in her chair. The fluid in her lungs kept her from lying down. The night of January 14th, I gave Marcia a pill to help her slee. I then went to bed. I lay awake for two hours, finally falling asleep. At 2:53 a.m. I awoke with Dr. Abraham's words ringing in my ears. Marcia had less than a month to live. I felt guilty that I was in our bed, but without her. My tears wouldn't stop.

The roller coaster was coming around the bend. It had been 17 years. Like a little boy in an amusement park, I did not want to get off the ride. Even though it was a tough ride, it was a ride that we shared. Now the journey's end was in sight.

Many thoughts ran through my mind that night. Her days were numbered. Who would she want to see? What would she want to do? Physically she couldn't do much. But mentally she was still strong. Inviting family and friends to visit seemed like the right thing to do.

I got up and poured Marcia's juice. Taking the juice and her pills from my hand, she said, "Didn't I tell you that you had to be strong?"
"Yeah, I think I am."
"I heard you during the night."
"Marcia, when you love someone, and you know that the Lord is close, it is so sad."
"You can't be a wimp," was her response.

CHAPTER 27

HERBAL MEDICINE

"God said, 'Behold, I have given you every herb bearing seed which is upon the face of all the earth."

Genesis 1:29

Back in the Fall of 2014, before our trip to Cleveland, a friend named Marty* had knocked on our door. "I heard that Marcia isn't doing very well," he told me. Marty was holding a bag. "Is it okay if I come in?" I invited him in.

"You know, New York State is talking about legalizing marijuana for medical purposes," Marty said. I had heard this in the news, but thought a doctor's prescription was needed. Marcia's eyes opened. She was listening attentively.

Opening the bag, Marty took out a strange contraption. Immediately, Marcia said, "I don't want to see this. Do what you have to do, but go into the other room." Marty and I walked away. He had to show me how to use the device.

He plugged it in and put the 'herb' in the top. I took a couple of puffs, and immediately started coughing and hacking. From the other room I could hear Marcia laughing. "Can't you handle it? You can leave this, but I don't think I'll use it."

Shortly after our January 14ᵗʰ Cleveland appointment, Marcia said, "I might try that thing." I looked at her.

"What do you mean? Try what?"

She answered, "What Marty brought."

"You're kidding!" I put the gadget on the table and plugged it in. Smoke was coming out of it when Marcia shook her head, "I can't do it. I just can't do it."

"Are you sure?"

"I just don't want to do it," she answered.

In his own way, Marty was only trying to help.

*Marty is not his real name.

CHAPTER 28

A SURPRISING QUESTION

"And the Lord God said, 'It is not good that the man should be alone. I will make a helper suitable for him."

Genesis 2:18

Ginny and Marcia, Myrtle Beach, South Carolina, 2004

Marcia was very close to her sister Ginny. On January 21st, Ginny and I were sitting with Marcia.

"Ginny, I need to ask you a question," Marcia said.
"Okay," Ginny said reluctantly.

"Ginny, put yourself in my position. If your husband Larry was going to be single soon, how would you feel if he dated or remarried?"

"Ginny," I said, "I am so relieved that she asked YOU that question, and not me!" We looked at each other and laughed.

Marcia said, "I am serious."

Ginny thought for a minute and said, "If Larry was happy with dating and ultimately remarrying, I'd understand."

Marcia looked at me and smiled. I think she wanted an honest answer. That's why she asked her sister. I jokingly asked Marcia, "Who would want me?" To which she responded, "Well, thanks a lot!"

CHAPTER 29

OLD FRIENDS

*"I have called you friends, for every-
thing that I learned from my Father I
have made known to you."*
                    John 15:15

We have been friends with three couples since the
1970's. Six or seven times a year we got together
at one of our homes for dinner. It was Mark and Carla
Stringer's turn to entertain. Mark called me and said, "I'll
bring all the food to your house tonight. That might be
easier for Marcia."

I said, "Thanks. That will help her. She won't have to leave
the house."

I told Marcia that everyone was coming over. "That wasn't
the plan," was her reply.
"I know. We thought it would be easier if everyone
came here."
"No, we're going to Mark and Carla's"
I was surprised that Marcia had the strength to travel. I
helped her get into the car, and in twenty minutes we were
at the Stringers.

Eleven days before heaven. Bottom row (L-R): Carla Prieur, Ginny Hallberg, Marcia and Carla Stringer. Top Row (L-R): Randy Prieur, Larry Hallberg, me and Mark Stringer, January 23, 2015

Marcia always said grace. On that night her prayer was poignant. She gave thanks for all of her friends. She went on to say, "No matter what happens, it is in your hands, Lord. Give the people here the strength to see you." There wasn't a dry eye in the room.

We were at the Stringers until midnight. No one wanted to go home until Marcia was ready to leave. Everyone agreed that January 23rd's dinner was the most memorable in our forty year history.

Good friends Jon and Maureen Stahley

CHAPTER 30

DINNER AND MOSES

*"In a little while you will see me no more,
and then after a little while you shall
see Me."*

John 16:16

M aureen Stahley called and asked if she and Jon could
stop over. I asked Marcia, "Would you like the Stahleys
to visit?" "Yes," she said. "Could they come tomorrow
night? Ask Maureen to bring macaroni and cheese with
ham." Maureen overheard the conversation and said, "Oh

my gosh, Kim. I don't know how to make that. It won't be as good as Marcia's."

"You have until tomorrow, January 27th to figure it out," I said. "See you then!"

After dinner Marcia said, "You're probably wondering why I wanted you here today." We all looked at each other as Marcia continued. "Here are the five songs I want sung at my Celebration of Life service." She handed us the paper.

Puzzled, the three of us looked at each other again. Marcia continued, "Kim, I want our flower girl, Rene, and Scotty, our ring bearer to read the Twenty-Third Psalm. Jon, I want you to tell funny stories at the end of the service. I want people to be smiling when they leave."

Not knowing what to think, Jon simply replied, "Oh my goodness." After a moment, Jon broke the silence. He said, "Let's play a little game, Marcia. Besides the Lord and your family, who would you like to meet first in Heaven?"

"Moses," Marcia quickly replied. "What a wonderful prophet he was."

We all laughed…partly from her response, and also as a way to ease our tension. We all learned a lot that night. Maureen learned how to make macaroni and cheese with ham. We knew the five songs Marcia selected for her Celebration of Life service. Jon needed to recite some humorous stories about the good old days. And Marcia… well, she was really anxious to meet Moses.

CHAPTER 31
FILLING IN FOR MARCIA

*"Blessed are the mourners for they shall
be comforted."*

Matthew 5:4

Julie Verdonik called us on January 29th. "How is Marcia doing today?" I answered, "Not great, Julie."

Julie told me that Lisa Crandall's sister had died suddenly from an infection. Lisa and Marcia were good friends who worked together for thirteen years. "Would you like to go to the funeral, Kim?" Julie asked.

"Yes, I would."

Marcia wanted to comfort her friend. She got out of her chair and said, "I'm going." "Marcia, you know you can't go." At that point, Marcia started to cry. "I'm going to go to the funeral home," she repeated.
"You're not strong enough, Marcia. I'll ask Ann Dahlberg to stay with you and I'll go in your place."
At the funeral home, Lisa asked about Marcia. I told her that she wasn't doing well. I expressed our sympathy, and Lisa simply said, "My sister's in Heaven now."

Later, when I got home, I told Marcia what Lisa had said about her sister being in Heaven. She replied, "I'll have to look her up."

My sister Marci and Marcia at a neighborhood wedding
in July 1971

Greg, Marcia and Ed,
summer of 1955

Marcia's engagement picture,
March 1973

My good friend Tim Carl sending us off on our
Florida honeymoon, July 28, 1973

Marcia and I headed to the military ball with the
Stahleys, November 1974

Toronto trip, April 1976

Long-time friends Bryan and Ann Dahlberg

Danielle's first day of school, September 1982

Jana Martin with Ryan and Marcia at Niagara Falls, summer of 1985

CHAPTER 32

YOUR WORK IS DONE

"Come to me, all you who labor and are heavy laden, and I will give you rest. Take my yoke upon you and learn from me, for I am gentle and lowly in heart, and you will find rest for your souls. For my yoke is easy and my burden is light."

Matthew 11:28-30

Marcia's friends Pam Secky and Judy Kraft visited her on January 29th. They were shocked by Marcia's appearance. She could barely open her right eye, and tumors had formed on her neck.

Marcia wanted Judy, a beautician, to cut her hair. The three girls talked and laughed as Marcia told Judy how to style her hair. She told her friends, "You know, I have the best husband and caregiver. He has given up so much to take care of me. There is no one else I'd rather have with me." We all wiped away our tears.

Marcia continued, "He's done so many good things for me, but his work is done."
"What do you mean my work is done?" I countered.
"Your work is done," Marcia repeated.

After Pam and Judy left, I thought about the words, 'Your work is done'. I think she wanted me to think about my future without her. She was deliberately pulling away from me.

Friends Pam Secky and Judy Kraft with Marcia in Buffalo at an indoor pro football game, April 2002

CHAPTER 33

YOU RAISE ME UP

*"You raise me up, so I can stand on
mountains."*

Josh Groban

Julie Verdonik emailed me a video on January 30th. The
Maple Grove Voices, a group of twenty-five students,
were singing Josh Groban's 'You Raise Me Up'. "Julie,
I've got to show this to Marcia," I said excitedly.

When I pushed the play button, Marcia said, "Oh, my
God!" The tears were in her eyes as she said, "This is one
of the songs I chose for my Celebration of Life service."
"I know. Julie is making you a copy of their CD."
"No, I don't want a CD," she replied. Confused, I asked why?
"Because I want them there. I want the Maple Grove
Voices to sing 'You Raise Me Up' at my Celebration of
Life service."

I got back to Julie. "Marcia watched the video and she
was really touched by it. However, I've got good news
and bad news."
"Give me the bad news first," she said quickly.
"She doesn't want the CD."
"She doesn't?"

"No," I replied. "She wants the Maple Grove Voices to sing the song at her celebration service.
Julie cried.

Julie called us later that day. All twenty-five students agreed to sing at Marcia's service. They considered it an honor.

CHAPTER 34

MARCIA AND SOPHIE

"Honor your father and mother so that you may live long in the land the Lord your God has given you."

Exodus 20:12

Sophie wanted to see Marcia. When she arrived, Marcia asked to be alone with her mom.

With Marcia in her brown chair, Sophie sat next to her. They held hands for forty-five minutes. I heard Marcia say, "Do you know the Lord, Mom?"

"Yes, I do. He's in my heart," said Sophie.

Marcia and Sophie, July 28, 1973

"I'm so happy," Marcia replied. They hugged each other and cried.

They talked about Heaven. Marcia said, "We'll be in Heaven together. It's a beautiful place. Heaven has colors we've never seen before."

"I look forward to being there with you," Sophie replied.

They both knew that this mother-daughter conversation was to be their last.

CHAPTER 35

MALYKS AND DEBBIE

"The Lord knows all human plans; He knows that they are futile."
Psalms 94:11

On January 31st, Ryan and Jordan helped me care for Marcia. She deferred to them when she needed something. She ignored my attempts to help her. Marcia asked her sons to invite our good friends Dave and Nancy Malyk and Debbie to dinner.

The boys left before our company arrived. We were talking and reminiscing when Nancy noticed my eyes closing. "Have you had a hard time sleeping, Kim?"
"I've only had a few hours of sleep in the last three days."
Nancy replied, "Kim, I'm staying with Marcia Monday night. I will be back Monday because you need sleep. Marcia wants you to rest."

Dave and I went for pizza while Debbie and Nancy stayed with Marcia. They helped her walk, and persuaded her to sip some wine. It didn't agree with her, so she quickly pushed it aside. That night, Marcia ate and drank very little. After dinner I asked if she was thirsty. She didn't answer. I repeated my question. Her eyes were closed, and she stayed silent.

Debbie Madl, Nancy and Dave Malyk

At my urging, Debbie asked, "Marcia, are you thirsty?" "Yes," she said. I asked Marcia if she wanted water or juice. She wouldn't acknowledge me. When Debbie asked her if she wanted some water, Marcia said yes.

Marcia ignored me again. It tore me apart. In her eyes, my work was done.

Everyone left at 9 o'clock. Ryan came back to help me care for his mother. We stayed up all night with her. I was angry. God needed to end my wife's suffering.

By morning I had come to terms with my anger. How could I be angry at God? He gave me the woman I'd loved for 45 years. He gave me Marcia who taught me all about faith, hope and love.

CHAPTER 36

I WANT TO GO HOME

"For this world is not our permanent home; we are looking forward to a home yet to come."

Hebrews 13:14

Marcia's strength was slipping fast. We sensed her body was slowing down. On three separate occasions, she talked about going home.

Danielle was by her mother's side when she woke up, looked around, and said, "I want to go home."
Danielle said, "Mom, you are home."
Marcia answered, "No, I'm not. I want to go home." When we told her that she was at home with us, she put her head down and closed her eyes.

While Ginny and I sat with Marcia, she said the same thing repeatedly. "I want to go home. I want to go home." When Ginny asked Marcia, "Where is that?", Marcia shook her head and repeated, "I want to go home; I want to go home."

Marcia said she wanted to go home when I was sitting with her. Her eyes were closed as she kept saying the words over and over again.

Marcia was longing for her permanent home in Heaven.

CHAPTER 37

I KNOW THAT VOICE

"A friend loves at all times."
Proverbs 17:17

Lisa Crandall and Nancy Risley called on February 2nd. Ryan told his mom that they wanted to visit. She whispered, "Okay."

Marcia didn't respond to her friends. She hadn't smiled or opened her eyes that day. As Nancy left, she tearfully said, "Marcia, I'm leaving. Goodbye."

Lisa and I were alone with Marcia. I told her, "There is something Marcia wants you to have."

Marcia with Lisa Crandall, December 21, 2014

It was one of two angels that were on her desk at school. My co-worker gave them to her in 2009 when she had stage four cancer. As Marcia cleared her desk the day she retired, she said to me, "Kim, I love these angels. Be sure to give one to Danielle, and the other to Lisa." I put the angel in Lisa's hand. We held hands and cried as we watched over Marcia.

Before Lisa left, she leaned over Marcia and said, "Do you know who this is?"
Marcia opened her eyes and looked at Lisa. She said, "I know that voice." Then she smiled.

We were shocked! We had heard Marcia's last words. We saw her last smile.

CHAPTER 38

THE KNOCK ON THE DOOR

"I have fought the good fight, I have fin-
ished the race, I have kept the faith."
2 Timothy 4:7

The evening of February 2nd, Nancy Malyk, our friend and a former Hospice caregiver, spent the night with Marcia. I went to bed and fell into a deep and much needed sleep.

Nancy played Christian music as Marcia struggled to breathe. Nancy spoke to Marcia, "You have to stay with me until morning. Kim needs his sleep. Your sons need to sleep. Stay with me, Marcia. Keep breathing. You're taking nine breaths every minute. Stay with me."

At 7:30 a.m., Nancy knocked on my bedroom door. "Kim, I think it's time for you to get up." I checked on Marcia. Then I called Ryan, Jordan and Marcia's family. I told them they needed to be by her side. I spoke quietly to Marcia. "The boys are on their way. Your brothers and sisters will be here soon. I'm here. You can go home now." Her breaths dropped to eight per minute, then down to seven.

Nancy left as our friend Sue Verbosky arrived. Marcia's brothers and sisters, Ryan, Jordan and I stood by her side. Sue told us that Marcia's breathing and pulse were slowing down. She then said, "Kim, I don't have a heartbeat anymore."

"She's in Heaven," I replied.
"Yes, she is," Sue said.

We were numb, but relieved. We were unbelievably sad, yet incredibly happy. Marcia's long fight was over. She finished the race. And throughout her struggles, she kept her faith.

Marcia died on her son Ryan's 36th birthday. Ryan refused to give in to grief. He said, "This day will be a double celebration. It's a celebration of my mom's life that she lived, and a celebration of when I was born. February 3rd is not a sad day; it is a great day!"

CHAPTER 39

THE FINAL GOODBYE

*"He heals the brokenhearted and binds
up their wounds."*

Psalm 147:3

Chip Johnson from Lind's Funeral Home helped us make arrangements. He knew that Marcia wanted to be cremated. He suggested that our family say their goodbyes that evening.

Sophie and the rest of Marcia's family gathered around her. She looked peaceful. She had a hint of a smile on her face. She was wearing her favorite pink vest.

I needed to be alone with her. I gently told her, "You were my rock for over forty years. I will continue to lean on you for strength until we meet again. I will tell others of your never-ending faith. I'm not sure how I'll do it, but I will."

I leaned over and tenderly kissed her goodbye.

CHAPTER 40

THE PINK LIGHT

"And those who are wise shall shine like the brightness of the sky above; and those who turn many to righteousness, like the stars forever and ever."
Daniel 12:3

The day that Dr. Ibaboa gave us the terrible news that Marcia must retire, we put a pink light bulb in the light on our porch. It was October, Breast Cancer Awareness Month. We turned it on every night.

On February 4th, the day after Marcia died, I felt completely abandoned. That evening I parked the car in the driveway, walked into the quiet house, and turned on the outside light. The pink light bulb had burned out. I sighed, went inside to get a 60 watt white bulb, and put it in the socket. I turned on the light, and its brilliance hurt my eyes. Puzzled, I took the pink bulb inside and glanced back at the porch light. The new light bulb's brightness had diminished.

I know that my 'Miracle Marcia' had just sent me a sign! Her suffering and cancer (pink light bulb) were over. The initial brilliance of the white light bulb told me that her new home was beyond her wildest expectations!

CHAPTER 41
CELEBRATION OF LIFE

"Death leaves a heartache no one can heal; love leaves a memory no one can steal."
Richard Puz, from an Irish headstone

Marcia requested that her funeral be a celebration of her life. She had a plan, and we were determined to follow her wishes.

On Saturday, February 7th, 350 people gathered at the Fluvanna Community Church. They listened to Kenny Rogers' 'Through The Years', as a picture presentation prepared by our 15 year old granddaughter, Alexandria, played across the screen. It beautifully captured Marcia's life.

As our family walked toward the front of the church, the Maple Grove Voices sang 'You Raise Me Up'. Our four oldest grandchildren led the procession. Alexandria held Marcia's urn. Michael held a framed picture of Marcia and me that was taken at his parent's wedding. Savannah carried her grandma's engagement photograph. Colby held a candle. Our three children and their spouses escorted me.

Pastor Mohl greeted the congregation and prayed. Scott and Renee, our ring bearer and flower girl 42 years ago, read the 23rd Psalm. Throughout the service, Kerry Byard and his family provided music that included Marcia's favorite hymns.

Danielle spoke to her mom with this poem, 'More Than a Mother' as it was read by her friend Meghan Gustafson Peterson:

More Than a Mother
When God set the world in place,
When He hung the stars up in space,
When He made the land and the sea,
Then He made you and me.

He sat back and saw all that was good,
He saw things to be as they should.
Just one more blessing He had in store;
He created a mother, but whatever for?

He knew a mother would have a special place
To shine His reflection on her child's face.
A mother will walk the extra mile
Just to see her children smile.

She'll work her fingers to the bone
To make a house into a home.
A mother is there to teach and guide;
A mother will stay right by your side.

She'll be there through your pain and strife,
She'll stay constant in your life.

A mother will lend a helping hand
Until you have the strength to stand.

She'll pick you up when you are down,
When you need a friend she'll stick around.
A mother is one who listens well,
Will keep her word, will never tell.

A mother never pokes or pries
But stands quietly by your side,
Giving you the strength you need,
Encouraging you to succeed.

A mother is one who can be strong
When you need someone to lean on;
You're more than a mother to me;
A reflection of Him in your face I see.

A love that knows no boundaries.
I'm glad that you chose to be
All this and more to me.

You share a love that knows no end,
You're more than my mother,
You are my friend.

Poem by Kari Keshmiry

Ryan was next to pay tribute to his mom. His heartfelt words were read by Pastor Dayle Keefer:

"First, I want to thank everyone for coming to my mom's Celebration of Life service. I also want to thank Pastor Keefer and the Fluvanna Community Church for hosting this special event.

My Mom passed away on February 3, 2015. I was born on February 3, 1979. This day the rest of my life will be a double celebration. It's a celebration of my mom's life that she lived, and a celebration of when I was born. February 3rd is not a sad day; it is a great day! Let us not cry; let us rejoice the day she went to Heaven to be with her Savior Jesus Christ.

Today we celebrate what my mom stands for and what she meant to everyone who is here. So I write to you, Mom…

The Letter To Mom

Mom,

Today I consider myself the luckiest man on the face of the earth. There is not enough time or words to say how lucky I am. Through these years that you battled this terrible disease, you showed so much strength, courage, and it makes me so proud to have been your son. You are an inspiration to everyone who you have touched. I thank God for you and Dad on the life you have directed for me.

Mom, the memories I have are so many, there is not enough time in the day, months, and years to tell everyone. I will share a few that are dear to me. One of the most important memories I have is when you took me to Wednesday night church in the village at Lakeside Bible Chapel. Dad was working third shift, so you would take Danielle and me to learn about God. I never knew then that going to church on Wednesday evening would shape my life the way it has. You did this because you thought this was the best for us, and I cannot appreciate that enough. I try to take those lessons that I have learned on Wednesday nights into my daily life. I commend you as a parent for doing this. Believing in Christ not only makes you a better person, it makes you humble, and it makes you complete. I will take this and apply it to my own family. This one important memory shaped my life and who I am today, and I thank you for it.

The other memory that is dear to me is the support you gave me at all of my athletic events. I was so proud to look up in the stands and see both my parents along with the Keefers, Verboskys and other parents supporting my friends and me. This made me feel so comforted knowing that my family and friends were supporting me. These attributes that God gave you, I will take with me for the rest of my life.

These memories last forever, Mom and as I look up to the sky, I will be reminded of these. So Mom, again, I say thank you.

Mom, I hope you do not mind that I took your reading glasses to work so every time I look at those glasses, you are looking at me and watching me.

Mom, no more pain; you do not have to worry about any scans coming back telling you the cancer has returned. You are healthy now, and you are in a better place. You deserve a better place. Dad, the stress is over, no more coming into my office and talking about Mom's health, and for you also no more worrying about how much cancer Mom has in her body. Take a deep breath, Dad, relax and enjoy the life God has put in front of you. Mom will be with you every step of the way. It is time for us now to create new memories that we will share.

Mom, this terrible disease may have taken your physical abilities away, but this disease will never touch your heart, your mind, your consideration for others and your love. I read you the scripture from 2 Timothy 4:7-8, 'I have fought the good fight, I have finished the race, and I have remained faithful. And now the prize awaits me – the crown of righteousness that the Lord, the righteous Judge, will give me on the great day of His return. And the prize is not just for me, but for all who eagerly look forward to His glorious return.' Mom, you have fought and you have won!! May God have a special place in His home for you, and someday I will see you again.

Thank you, Mom. You did good; you did real good! I love you with all my heart!

Your son Ryan, born on 'Miracle Marcia' Day.

Ryan Rambacher

Jordan remembered his mom with the poem, 'Quiet Moments'. David Oste read the poem for Jordan.

Quiet Moments

When I was young I used to love to sit upon your knee.
I'd gaze into your loving eyes as your arms enfolded me.
Your gentle kiss would stir the golden tendrils of my hair,
As whispered sentiments of love we quietly would share.
We'd read a book together, the same time after time.
I knew all of the words by heart, you didn't seem to mind.
When darkness fell, you tucked me in and gently kissed my cheek.
You'd wish upon a shooting star the Lord my soul to keep.
The years have passed so quickly, death parted you from me.
I hope you know how much it meant when I sat upon your knee.
Gazing to the heavens, as I quietly reminisce,

I'd give a million of those stars to feel your gentle kiss.
I'd give all my tomorrows to hear you read to me,
And remember those quiet moments when I sat upon
your knee.

Poem by Louisa Lodge

I listened to the tender words my children spoke to their mother. I took a deep breath and walked to the front of the church. As I stood behind the pulpit, I looked out at the tearful crowd of friends and relatives. I definitely needed to interject some humor. I reached under the pulpit, grabbed a box of tissues, slapped it down and said, "A few weeks ago I told Marcia that I'd speak at her Celebration of Life service." She laughed and said, "You'll never get through it, Kim."
I replied, "I will do it Marcia. I'll bet you I can do it."
"Okay," she said. "It's a bet!"
"This is for you, Marcia."

"Marcia and I thank you for being here today. We also thank you for your prayers over the last seventeen years. You know what Marcia would say if she saw all this? She would ask, 'Don't you people have anything better to do?'

"Many people who are here today have given a standing ovation for good performances in a play, and a baseball, football or basketball game. We give standing ovations for those who achieve their goals.

"Over the years I saw the best athlete I've ever known hit more home runs, sink more three-point baskets, and kick more field goals than both of our sons. Yes, Marcia was a highly decorated athlete. It was evident in her determination, perseverance, strength and optimism. She wanted to win, and hated to lose. Marcia was an athlete of life, and she won.

"Oh, wait…I might need these!" (I put a second box of tissues on the pulpit.)

"When Marcia marched into an enormous stadium last Tuesday, there were hundreds of thousands on their feet. They gave her the greatest standing ovation of her life. Leading that cheer was our Captain and King, the Lord Jesus Christ. He adorned her with crowns and handed her dozens of trophies.

"Through her illness, cancer didn't destroy her smile, her sense of humor, her beauty or her optimistic outlook.

"Cancer didn't eliminate her kindness or her love for her family, her children and her grandchildren.

"Cancer didn't diminish her compassion for her coworkers at Maple Grove High School, and her countless friends.

"Cancer didn't take away her fight to live.

"Cancer didn't take away her faith, her salvation, or her love of Jesus Christ.

"In closing, I need to tell Marcia something...

"Marcia Frances, I won the bet. I plan to collect the next time I see you. I love you."

It was Marcia's hope that her family and friends would leave her service smiling, as they remembered her. True to his word, Jon Stahley's sense of humor was evident as he recalled the 'Good Old Days'...

Jon:

"Yes, Martin Kim Rambacher (MKR) lived across the street from Maureen and me. He hailed from Stow, Ohio. How often did Kim tell us that Stow was the hometown of Larry Czonka, and it was located right next to the NFL Hall of Fame in Canton?

"Back in the '70's Kim looked like a cross between the old comedian and movie critic Gene Shalit and the Frito Bandito! He was a very white guy, sporting a big black Afro in which a mother bird could make a fine nest, and he had a cheesy little mustache. Lastly, he was a rabid Cleveland Indians baseball fan who had moved into New York Yankees territory.

"We all lived in 'the hood', which was a few blocks in Bemus Point. Our common denominators were lots of kids...and poverty. Since we had no money, we were forced to do home and auto repairs ourselves. Well, MKR had the cutest set of tools you've ever seen. His little hammer and three other tools were snugly nestled in a little plastic box that could have served as a girl's sewing kit. So you can only imagine his lack of talent when it came to home maintenance.

"There was a standard dialogue that Marcia and Kim would have when admonishing one another. While partially giving the evil eye to Kim, Marcia would say in an aggravating, slightly whiney way, "Keeeiim!" She would draw out his name like that. Kim would furl his eyebrows and quickly say in a gruff voice, "Marcia Frances?" So, for years when we heard "Keeeiim" or "Marcia Frances", we knew a spat had begun.

"I fondly remember the day that Marcia decided to wash the storm windows. An extension ladder was borrowed, of course, and extended up to the second story window of their small home. Now, you need to keep in mind that MKR was one of the main firefighters in the Bemus Point Volunteer Fire Department. He was well trained and fearless when crawling into and onto burning buildings. However, this same fearlessness did not translate to home maintenance. Quietly and quickly, I positioned myself to peek around the corner of the house. I didn't want to miss this one!

"Marcia was well along with child at this time. Much conversation transpired between the two of them at the base of the ladder. Finally, the man of the house began his ascent ever so slowly. With a death grip, he held onto the ladder with one hand, and held the cleaning tools in the other. By now MKR's black glasses were crooked and he was sweating profusely. Then it started. "Keeeiim, just get up there. Hurry up." This elicited a "Marcia Frances, I know." Kim was holding on desperately, and he was only on the second rung. Finally Marcia told him to come down and, you guessed it… the very pregnant lady of the house went up the ladder to wash the windows. When Korcyl, as I called her, wanted something done, it got done!

"One Saturday Kim and I decided to build picnic tables. Since our houses were right across the street from each other, MKR didn't have to get his tools dirty. Marcia decided to go shopping for the day, and MKR was also assigned the duty of watching his baby daughter, Danielle. I'm sure Marcia's instructions were very specific and repeated several times prior to her departure. Kim did watch Danielle, but that's all he did…watched her. He placed her stroller in close proximity to us, and that was it. Danielle sat there…and sat there…and sat there as she watched her dad build a picnic table. At one point, I said to MKR, "Hey Kim, don't you have to do something to her once in a while?" He glanced at Danielle and said, "Nawww. She's fine."

"When Marcia returned, she pulled into the driveway, took the packages into the house, then immediately came back outside to check on her entrusted first child. "Keeeiim, look at her!" was the exclamation from the distraught mother. An 'ooze' was expanding to the stroller and probably onto the ground. Marcia then huffed across the street with her heavily soiled first born.

"Yes, we had a lot of good times. We each had three children, and as the years went by, we grew closer to each other. Our Lord and Savior Jesus Christ was gracious enough to save Kim, Marcia, Maureen and me. This added a whole new dimension to our lifelong friendship.

"Marcia is looking down from heaven today. She's smiling as she says, "They really did it up right, didn't they Moses?"

CHAPTER 42

THE BRACELET

*"God hides his most precious treasures
for his saints in their most difficult and
painful experiences."*
'Things Not Seen" - Jon Bloom

On Christmas Eve, 2014. Danielle, Ryan, Jordan and I were frantically searching the house. Curious, Marcia asked, "What are you doing?" "Oh," I said. "We lost something."

When Danielle came home for Thanksgiving, she bought a Pandora charm bracelet for her mother. She left it at our house, knowing that she would return for Christmas. "I put it right here in the bedroom," Danielle said. She was upset because we couldn't locate it, and it was too late to buy her mother another Christmas present. "Dad, what happened to it? It was in a green box."

"I never saw it," I said.

Our one-story small home was uncluttered. How could we lose a jewelry box?

On Christmas morning Danielle promised to replace the bracelet. She would give it to her mom when we got together in Kiawah. Marcia smiled at Danielle and said, "Oh, don't worry about it." For some reason, Danielle never bought a replacement.

On February 8th, the day after Marcia's Celebration of Life service, Danielle and her children Alexandria and Colby, were ready to fly back to Charlotte. "I'm checking the house to be sure that I have everything," Danielle told me. Then I heard Danielle scream, "Oh, my God!"
"What's wrong?" I asked.
"Dad, come in here!" she said.
On top of the dresser, in front of Marcia's urn was the missing green Pandora box. Dumbfounded, we all stared at it.

I broke the silence and said, "Okay, Danielle, did you put it there?" "No, Dad," she said in astonishment.

The night before, I had put Marcia's cell phone in front of her urn. There was no box on the dresser. That morning the cell phone was on top of the bracelet box. We shook our heads. We couldn't imagine how the lost box reappeared overnight.

Danielle opened the box and gave the bracelet to Alexandria. We knew that's what Marcia would want us to do.

CHAPTER 43

NO MORE SICK DAYS

"Let each of you look not only to his own interests; but also to the interests of others."

Philippians 2:4

Back during our New Year's vacation in Kiawah, we received a call from Nancy Risley, an administrator at Bemus Point Central School. What she said surprised us and spoke to our hearts. We learned about the generosity of friends and colleagues who offered to help Marcia in a very practical way. Nancy phoned to tell us that some of the school's employees donated 55 of their sick days to Marcia. "Why would they give away their sick days to another sick person?", Marcia asked with tears in her eyes.

In January, shortly after we returned from Kiawah, Marcia said, "Keeiim, I want you to go to the high school and talk to Nancy right now."

"Why do you want me to go?"

"You need to ask her what will happen if I don't use all of the donated sick days. Will my friends get them back?"

"Marcia," I said, "It's 8:30 in the morning and it's snowing and blowing. Can't it wait?"

"No, I want to know now," she replied.

Reluctantly I went to the school, entered Nancy's office, and told her that Marcia had a question for her. "She wants to know what will happen to the donated sick days if she doesn't use them? Will they go back to the people who gave them to her?"

Nancy looked at me and said, "Kim, we've never had this situation before. I'll have to get back to you."

When I got home, Marcia was sound asleep in her chair. When she woke up, the first thing she said was, "What's the answer?" I told her that Nancy didn't have an answer, but she would get back to us. Marcia looked at me, gave me that beautiful smile, nodded 'Yes', and said, "Okay."

On February 9th, two days after Marcia's Celebration of Life service, I was at the high school signing insurance forms. I asked Nancy how many of the 55 donated days Marcia had used. With tears in her eyes, she said, "Marcia's own sick days ended on February 3rd, the very day she died. She never had to use any of the donated days."

Thinking back to that January day, I now understand Marcia's smile, the nod, and the reassuring 'okay'. It was as if she planned events so that she would not use any of the donated days. As for the answer to Marcia's question, the donated days were returned to her co-workers.

CHAPTER 44

THE BOY IN THE HALL

"Then your Father who sees what is done in secret, will reward you."
Matthew 6:6

After leaving Nancy's office, a student approached me. I didn't know him. Our eyes met, and he said, "Mr. Rambacher, I miss your wife."

"Thank you," I said.

He explained, "She always gave me lunch money when I needed it."

I replied, "Oh my goodness. That's why I don't have any money!" We both laughed.

When I told Julie Verdonik about this conversation, she said to me, "Kim, Marcia often gave lunch money to other students."

"Really? I guess I'm not surprised. Marcia was always there to lend a helping hand."

CHAPTER 45

MARCIA'S FRAGRANCE

"You have to give us a sign."

Ginny

Years ago Ginny picked up Marcia and the two sisters went shopping. When Marcia got in the car, Ginny said, "What perfume are you wearing? I love it!"

"It's 'Twilight Woods'." From that day on, Ginny and Marcia both wore 'Twilight Woods'.

Weeks before Marcia's death, Ginny said to her, "You'll have to give us signs, Marcia. We have to know you are in heaven watching over us."

On February 12th, Ginny was at work. She left her office for a few minutes. When she returned, her office was filled with the scent of 'Twilight Woods'. Ginny immediately called me. "Kim, you won't believe this! I left my office, and when I got back the room smelled like 'Twilight Woods'. I don't wear perfume to work. I checked the perfume bottle I carry in my purse. The cap was in place and the bottle wasn't broken. The scent was really strong for a minute, and then it suddenly disappeared. I know I didn't imagine this. I think Marcia sent me a sign!"

CHAPTER 46

MOSES!

*"Having therefore obtained help of God,
I continue unto this day, witnessing
both to small and great."*

Acts 26:22

Danielle and her family were back in Charlotte. She and Alexandria were in church on Sunday, February 15th. Her pastor had been discussing the Book of Luke with his congregation. He announced, "You all know that we've been studying Luke. But we're going to take a break. We'll get back to Luke next week. Today I woke up and felt the need to speak about Moses."

Danielle and Alexandria looked at each other with tears in their eyes. They knew that Marcia wanted to meet Moses in Heaven. After the service, Danielle called me and said, "Dad, you won't believe what happened in church today!" She told me the story.

"Well, Danielle, it seems to me that Mom is looking down on you. Two signs in one week!"

Maple Grove students and faculty dressed in pink and purple in
remembrance of Marcia

CHAPTER 47

GOODBYE FRIEND

*"How lucky I am to have something that
makes saying goodbye so hard."*
Winnie The Pooh

The following tribute was printed in the March 2015
Bemus Point School District's newsletter. Pictured next
to the article were Maple Grove's 200 students. They were
all dressed in pink and purple in remembrance of Marcia.

Through her various stages of cancer, seven types of chemotherapy, and a hairless head covered by a hat, Marcia rarely missed a day of work. She is missed by her friends, colleagues and students.

It is with heavy hearts that the Bemus Point Central School District said goodbye to a beloved member of its family on February 3, 2015.

Mrs. Rambacher was a 1970 Maple Grove graduate who then went on to be employed by the district for 30 years. During her employment, she worked as a teacher's aide, library assistant, and most recently was the attendance clerk at Maple Grove.

Mrs. Rambacher will be remembered as a courageous and compassionate woman who always had a smile on her face. She will be missed by the Bemus Point community.

> *Goodbyes are not forever.*
> *Goodbyes are not the end.*
> *They simply mean I'll miss you*
> *Until we meet again. – Author unknown*

CHAPTER 48
'MIRACLE MARCIA' SCHOLARSHIP

"Apply thine heart unto instruction, and thine ears to the words of knowledge."
Proverbs 23:12

Our family established a scholarship in memory of Marcia. She always rooted for the underdog. Consequently, the scholarship recipient would be a hard-working goal-oriented student with above average grades.

A committee nominated three students who met the scholarship criteria. After carefully reviewing their profiles, I chose a young lady who wanted to study dance. She hoped to dance on Broadway.

The committee told me I made an excellent choice. When I was shown a picture of the winner, I immediately recognized her. She sang with the Maple Grove Voices at Marcia's service. During the performance, she caught my eye. We were both terribly sad, but we smiled at each other.

At the awards dinner I introduced Madeline Jones, the first 'Miracle Marcia' Scholarship winner. We both cried. I know Marcia would approve of Maddie who is currently studying dance at the State University of New York in Purchase, New York.

The first "Miracle Marcia Rambacher Scholarship"
recipient, Madeline "Maddie" Jones

CHAPTER 49

THE WHITE ROSE

"The intricate and elegant rose offers a glimpse of a masterful Creator's active presence in creation."
Unknown

The night before Marcia's Celebration of Life service, one of Marcia's coworkers asked me, "What was Marcia's favorite flower?" I immediately answered, "White roses."

I later learned that Marcia's Maple Grove coworkers had a plan. Art teacher Kevin Johnson designed a stained glass panel.

In the fall of 2015, I was invited to the dedication of this work of art. The beautiful white rose in the stained glass panel now hangs in the office window behind Marcia's desk. Beneath the rose are the words, 'In Memory of Marcia Rambacher'.

Every time I walk across the parking lot towards the entrance of Maple Grove High School, I glance at the office windows. There hangs the stained glass white rose, reminding everyone of 'Miracle Marcia'.

Maple Grove High School principal Julie Verdonic and art teacher
Kevin Johnson stand next to the stained glass panel (designed by Kevin)
in the high school office window

CHAPTER 50

CLEVELAND INDIANS FANTASY CAMP

"In your presence is fullness of joy; In your right hand there are pleasures forever."

Psalm 16:11

In the summer of 2014, Marcia and I watched a Cleveland Indians baseball game. We both followed the Indians. Marcia especially liked Rick Manning, the team's current announcer and a former Indians all-star player. During the game, a commercial advertised their Fantasy Camp at the team's training facility in Goodyear, Arizona.

"Geezee-peezee," I said. "I would love to go to that!"
Marcia responded, "Kim, you'll get there someday."

That someday came true. I attended Fantasy Camp in January 2016. Rick Manning was one of the coaches and the camp's director. Decked out in my Cleveland Indians uniform, and wearing pink armbands in memory of Marcia, Rick and I had our picture taken. Marcia was right...I made it!

All-Star Cleveland Indians centerfielder Rick Manning and me at fantasy
camp in Goodyear, Arizona, January 20, 2016

AUTHOR'S NOTES

"Love one another with brotherly affection. Outdo one another in showing honor."
Romans 12:10

If I had a nickel for every time someone asked me how Marcia was feeling, I'd be a rich man. Marcia said to me, "Kim, our friends have done so much for us. We haven't done anything for them. That's not fair! When this is over, you've got to remember our friends."

After Marcia passed, I remembered her request. I made a list of several friends who were close to us over the last seventeen years. I paid back their kindness with dinners, breakfasts, and flowers. As I was thanked, I always said, "This one's on Marcia."

I invited a group of friends to my house for a steak dinner on June 13th. Earl and Ginger Johnson, Jim and Cheryl Shephard, and Debbie Madl all had a great time. After dinner we sat and reminisced.

I had originally planned a surprise birthday/retirement party for Marcia on June 13th. My friend Steve Ehmke is a disc jockey for a country music radio station in Tampa. Steve was instrumental in planning a ten minute video that would've played at the party. Kenny Rogers had agreed to send a personal message to Marcia. He then planned to sing, 'Through the Years' to her. Having those five people around me that evening helped me cope with the sadness I felt over what would have happened on June 13th if Marcia was still alive.

I've gone out with our group that's been together for forty years. One time Mark and Carla, Carla and Randy, and Ginny and Larry got together with me to celebrate my retirement. There was a strange feeling of loss. There were always eight of us, and now we needed a table for seven. The table remained eight because of the empty chair beside me.

At our last gathering I simply picked up the empty chair and carried it across the room. When I returned to the table, my friends sadly looked at me. It was their loss too. They were aware of the empty chair. I think Marcia would understand why I moved that chair.

People say I'm different. I'm still me. I love people. I'm funny. I smile. I love sports. I realize that life goes on. However, without Marcia, it's easier said than done.

As I reflect on my love for Marcia, I realize I sometimes took our time together for granted. During our 42 years of marriage, there was so much laughter, and countless unforgettable moments. How I long for those days. I miss holding Marcia in my arms.

I hope that everyone who reads Marcia's marvelous story is inspired by her strength and courage. Though we lost her on February 3, 2015, I believe that her message will continue to bring people to the Lord.

With only eight days remaining in her life, Marcia told me, "We've had a lot of great memories, Kim. When my life is over, you have to make new memories on your own." At the time I couldn't grasp the meaning of her words. Now I understand what she meant. I have followed her advice. Life goes on, and I have made some wonderful new memories as I move forward without her.

Though she is not here, she will never be forgotten. Simply put, "You were my miracle, Marcia. I love you."

Looking out to the future, May 17, 2015

I WOULD LIKE TO ACKNOWLEDGE:

- ❖ Dr. Jairus Y. Ibaboa and Margaret DiDominico from Jamestown Medical Oncology. Your professionalism and sense of humor were appreciated.
- ❖ Dr. Abraham and Nurse Nancy Dalpiaz from Cleveland Clinic
- ❖ Cancer Treatment Centers of America – Chicago, Illinois
- ❖ WCA Hospital
- ❖ Jamestown Post Journal – Scott Kindberg
- ❖ Quick Solutions Printing – Bev Johnson
- ❖ Lind Funeral Home – Chip Johnson
- ❖ Pastor Clyde and Linda Mohl, and Marcia's Lakeside Bible Chapel 'family'
- ❖ Bemus Point Central School District employees and students
- ❖ Judy Hall, longtime friend and coworker

❖ Cummins Inc. for understanding that being with Marcia was a necessity

❖ True friends Marcia Nolan Schultz, Jim and Cheryl Shephard, Scott and Brenda Lewellen, Cindy Davin, and Ned and Ro Ward. They listened to Marcia's miracles and encouraged me to write this book.

❖ Sheila Morton, Big Al Miller, Ken Perry, Ed Miller, Alberto Rodriguez, Matt Fehlman, Charley Bonita, Dale Tremblay, Tammy Stanton and Emily Simmons, my friends and coworkers at Cummins

❖ Riley Olmstead, for all of the food

❖ Brian and Maria Berube who believed that Marcia was their living angel.

❖ Whitney and Marlene Lundgren whose prayers were appreciated.

❖ Floyd and Becky Prine for caring.

❖ Rita and Ron Fishel, Rita's memory quilts are magnificent.

❖ Words With Friends mate, Peter Weckerle from Adelaide, South Australia

❖ Thom and Cheryl Shagla

❖ Terry and Bud May whose prayers were felt daily.

❖ Ade Humbert, proof reader extraordinaire

❖ Our friend (who wishes to remain anonymous) for typing the final copy.

A portion of the proceeds from this book
will be donated to:

Breast Cancer Awareness

Pastor Clyde and Linda Mohl's Retirement Fund

'Miracle Marcia' Rambacher Scholarship Fund

Hospice of Chautauqua County, Inc.

My best man Denny Martin and wife Jana,
February 2016

Church outing in Pittsburgh, PA with Pat
Madonia and Peggy Swanson, Spring 1997

Marcia with her first wig – she loved it!!
March 1999

Miami Dolphins hall-of-fame linebacker Nick Buoniconti at the annual banquet for the Miami Project to Cure Paralysis. Marcia and I were his guests for the volunteer work we did in Western New York on behalf of the Buoniconti fund.

With Dana at Margaritaville Restaurant
in Myrtle Beach, 2002

Piggyback ride for Alexandria, February 2004

One of the dozen trips to Myrtle Beach, April 2007

The Korcyl family at Sophie's 90th birthday party, front row (L-R): Ed, Sophie and Tom. Back Row (L-R): Marcia, Sue, Lanny, Greg, Janice and Ginny. July 2008

Our family two weeks after stage 4 reappeared. Front row (L-R) Me holding Colby; Alexandria, and Marcia holding Michael. Back row (L-R) Danielle, Pete, Jordan, Ardelle, Ryan and Katie. November 2009

Our good friends Chip and Cindy Swanson with me and Marcia at their
daughter Jamie's wedding, July 28, 2012

Jordan, Marcia and Ryan at Sophie's watching the Bills win>!@#$%?
September 2012

BOOK BIOGRAPHIES AND CREDITS

Patricia Pihl is a personal historian and founder of Real Life Legacies, which helps individuals preserve their stories and memories in beautiful books. Pat works with individuals who value their unique experiences and heritage, assisting them through interview and creation of first person narratives. A member of the Association of Personal Historians, she believes her work helps to "save lives one story at a time."

Patricia Pihl,
Lead Writer

Pat is also author of "Lost Places of Chautauqua County." To learn ways to preserve your story and why doing so is important, contact her at pat@reallifelegacies.com or visit www.reallifelegacies.com. Pat lives in Mayville, New York with her husband David, sons Will and Stephen and their dog, Beckham.

Rene McCann, Graphic
Designer, Cover

As an award winning Senior Art Director/Creative Lead, René McCann has executed design projects for multi-million dollar advertising campaigns. She has played a major role in promoting the growth and success of every company for which she created work. She has developed and maintained brand standards, Point-Of-Purchase displays, animated video presentations, and compelling trade show designs from 3D structures, to touchscreen dealer tools and in-store kiosks, websites and collateral. Her 20+ years of experience and expertise has given her a positive reputation of someone who is highly sought after.

René is a mother of twin boys, married and lives in Kent, Ohio.

Cheryl Shephard, Editor

Cheryl Shephard is a retired elementary school teacher. She has published a cookbook and is currently writing a children's book. Cheryl and her husband, Jim, live in Bemus Point, New York and Fort Myers, Florida. The Shephards and their five children are friends of the Rambachers.